C000141884

In the same series

THE LITTLE BOOK OF ANGELS

✦

THE LITTLE BOOK OF CELTIC WISDOM

✦

THE LITTLE BOOK OF IRON JOHN

THE

Little Book

— OF —

THE BIBLE

ELEMENT
Shaftesbury, Dorset ✦ Rockport, Massachusetts
Brisbane, Queensland

BLESSED BE THE NAME OF THE LORD

ALL THINGS ARE FULL OF LABOUR

This compilation © John Baldock 1993

Published in Great Britain in 1993 by
ELEMENT BOOKS LIMITED
Longmead, Shaftesbury, Dorset

Published in the USA in 1993 by
ELEMENT, INC
42 Broadway, Rockport, MA 01966

Published in Australia in 1993 by
ELEMENT BOOKS LIMITED
for JACARANDA WILEY LIMITED
33 Park Road, Milton, Brisbane, 4064

Cover illustration: Detail from Chartres Cathedral

Designed and produced by
BRIDGEWATER BOOKS

Printed and bound in Hong Kong by Excel Graphic Arts
British Library Cataloguing in Publication data available

Library of Congress Cataloging in Publication data available

ISBN 1-85230-447-2

FOR I AM SICK WITH LOVE

A TIME TO DIE, A TIME TO BE BORN

BLESSED ARE THE MERCIFUL

FOR WE ARE INDEED HIS OFFSPRING

FOREWORD

A midst the constant hustle and bustle of our daily lives there arise certain moments when we feel the need to pause and collect our thoughts or to seek inspiration of a spiritual kind. This little anthology has been compiled with such moments in mind, providing material for contemplation and consolation that will uplift the heart and feed the soul. Intended to appeal to readers of all faiths, its pages gather together some of the most poetic and inspiring passages from the Bible – ranging from the opening words of Genesis to the mystical vision of the Book of Revelation, from the passionate poetry of the Song of Solomon to the parables of Jesus. These passages have also been selected to reflect the recurring Biblical themes of love and light, the mysterious workings of the Spirit, the wonder of the Creation, and the soul's quest for wisdom and understanding and, ultimately, for the experience of union with God.

In general the order of the quotations follows that of the books of the Bible, but their choice and arrangement is such that the reader may dip into them at random or read through the book progressively, from cover to cover.

JOHN BALDOCK
Ascension Day 1993

I N the beginning God created the heavens and the earth.

The earth was without form and void, and darkness was upon the face of the deep; and the Spirit of God was moving over the face of the waters.

And God said, "Let there be light"; and there was light. ←

Then God said, "Let us make man in our image, after our likeness …

So God created man in his own image, in the image of God he created him; male and female he created them.

And God blessed them, and God said to them, "Be fruitful and multiply…" ←

GENESIS *1:1-3, 26, 27-28* [RSV]

HE LORD our God is one LORD; and you shall love the LORD your God with all your heart, and with all your soul, and with all your might. ✦

"This commandment which I command you this day is not too hard for you, neither is it far off. It is not in heaven, that you should say, 'Who will go up for us to heaven, and bring it to us, that we may hear it, and do it?' Neither is it beyond the sea, that you should say, 'Who will go over the sea for us, and bring it to us, that we may hear it and do it?' But the word is very near you; it is in your mouth and in your heart, so that you can do it." ✦

DEUTERONOMY 6:4; 30:11-14 [RSV]

AKED I came from my mother's womb, and naked shall I return; the LORD gave, and the LORD has taken away; blessed be the name of the LORD." ←

JOB *1:21* [RSV]

S the hart panteth after
the water brooks,
So panteth my soul after
thee, O God.
My soul thirsteth for God,
for the living God. ←

PSALM *42:1-2* [AV]

THE LORD is my shepherd;
I shall not want.
He maketh me to lie down in
green pastures:
   he leadeth me beside the still waters.
He restoreth my soul:
   he leadeth me in the paths
   of righteousness
   for his name's sake.
Yea, though I walk through the valley of
the shadow of death,
   I will fear no evil:
   for thou art with me;
   thy rod and thy staff they comfort me.
Thou preparest a table before me
   in the presence of mine enemies:
   thou anointest my head with oil;
   my cup runneth over.
Surely goodness and mercy shall follow me
   all the days of my life:
   and I will dwell in the house
   of the LORD for ever. ⬅

PSALM 23 | AV |

LORD, thou hast searched me
and known me!
Thou knowest when I sit down and when
I rise up;
    thou discernest my thoughts from afar.
Thou searchest out my path and my
lying down,
    and art acquainted with all my ways.
Even before a word is on my tongue,
    lo, O LORD, thou knowest it altogether.
Thou dost beset me behind and before,
    and layest thy hand upon me.
Such knowledge is too wonderful for me;
    it is high, I cannot attain it. ←

Whither shall I go from thy Spirit?
    Or whither shall I flee from thy presence?
If I ascend to heaven, thou art there!
    If I make my bed in Sheol, thou
art there!
If I take the wings of the morning
    and dwell in the uttermost parts of
the sea,
even there thy hand shall lead me,
    and thy right hand shall hold me.

EVEN THERE THY HAND SHALL LEAD ME

AND THY RIGHT HAND SHALL HOLD ME

If I say, "Let only darkness cover me,
    and the light about me be night,"
even the darkness is not dark to thee;
    the night is bright as the day;
    for darkness is as light with thee.
For thou didst form my inward parts,
    thou didst knit me together in my
mother's womb.
I praise thee, for thou art fearful
and wonderful.
    Wonderful are thy works!
Thou knowest me right well;
    my frame was not hidden from thee,
    when I was being made in secret,
    intricately wrought in the depths
of the earth.
Thy eyes beheld my unformed substance;
    in thy book were written, every one
of them,
    the days that were formed for me,
    when as yet there was none of them.
How precious to me are thy thoughts,
O God!
    How vast is the sum of them! ←

PSALM *139:1-17* [RSV]

WONDERFUL ARE THY WORKS

THOU KNOWEST ME RIGHT WELL

HOM the LORD loveth he
correcteth;
Even as a father the son in whom
he delighteth.
Happy is the man that findeth wisdom,
And the man that getteth understanding.
For the merchandise of it is better than
the merchandise of silver,
And the gain thereof than fine gold.
She is more precious than rubies:
And all the things thou canst desire
are not to be compared unto her.
Length of days is in her right hand;
And in her left hand riches and honour.
Her ways are ways of pleasantness,
And all her paths are peace.
She is a tree of life to them that lay hold
upon her:

And happy is every one that retaineth her.
The LORD by wisdom hath founded
the earth;
By understanding hath he established
the heavens. ←

*W*isdom is the principal thing; therefore
get wisdom:
And with all thy getting get understanding.
Exalt her, and she shall promote thee:
She shall bring thee to honour, when thou
dost embrace her.
She shall give to thine head an ornament
of grace:
A crown of glory shall she deliver to thee. ←

PROVERBS 3:12-19; 4:7-9 [AV]

OR she is a breath of the power of God,

and a pure emanation of the glory of the Almighty;

therefore nothing defiled gains entrance into her.

For she is a reflection of eternal light,

a spotless mirror of the working of God,

and an image of his goodness.

Though she is but one, she can do all things,

and while remaining in herself, she renews all things;

in every generation she passes into holy souls

and makes them friends of God, and prophets;

for God loves nothing so much

as the man who lives with wisdom.

For she is more beautiful than the sun,
  and excels every constellation of
the stars. ←

*S*he reaches mightily from one end of
the earth to the other,
  and she orders all things well.
I loved her and sought her from
my youth,
  and I desired to take her for my bride,
  and I became enamoured of
her beauty.
She glorifies her noble birth by living
with God,
  and the Lord of all loves her.
For she is an initiate in the knowledge
of God,
  and an associate in his works. ←

WISDOM OF SOLOMON *6:12-13, 17-20;*
7:25-29; 8:1-4 [RSV]

THE GLORY OF THE ALMIGHTY

ANITY of vanities, saith the Preacher, vanity of vanities; all is vanity. What profit hath a man of all his labour which he taketh under the sun? One generation passeth away, and another generation cometh: but the earth abideth for ever. The sun also ariseth, and the sun goeth down, and hasteth to his place where he arose. The wind goeth toward the south, and turneth about unto the north;

VANITY OF VANITIES

ALL THINGS ARE FULL OF LABOUR

it whirleth about continually, and the wind returneth again according to his circuits. All the rivers run into the sea; yet the sea is not full; unto the place from whence the rivers come, thither they return again. All things are full of labour; man cannot utter it: the eye is not satisfied with seeing, nor the ear filled with hearing. The thing that hath been, it is that which shall be; and that which is done is that which shall be done: and there is no new thing under the sun. Is there any thing whereof it may be said, See, this is new? it hath been already of old time, which was before us. There is no remembrance of former things; neither shall there be any remembrance of things that are to come with those that shall come after. ←

ECCLESIASTES *1:2-11* [AV]

O every thing there is a season,
and a time to every purpose under
the heaven:
a time to be born, and a time to die;
a time to plant, and a time to pluck up
that which is planted;
a time to kill, and a time to heal;
a time to break down, and a time to
build up;
a time to weep, and a time to laugh;
a time to mourn, and a time to dance;
a time to cast away stones, and a time to
gather stones together;
a time to embrace, and a time to refrain
from embracing;
a time to get, and a time to lose;
a time to keep, and a time to cast away;
a time to rend, and a time to sew;
a time to keep silence, and a time
to speak;
a time to love, and a time to hate;
a time of war, and a time of peace. ←

ECCLESIASTES 3:1-8 [AV]

THEN shall the dust return to the earth as it was: and the spirit shall return unto God who gave it. Vanity of vanities, saith the preacher; all is vanity.

...Of making many books there is no end: and much study is a weariness of flesh. Let us hear the conclusion of the whole matter: Fear God, and keep his commandments: for this is the whole duty of man. ❖

ECCLESIASTES *12:7-13* [AV]

THOUGH we speak much we cannot reach the end,
and the sum of our words is:
"He is the all."
Where shall we find strength to praise him?

For he is greater than all his works. ←

ECCLESIASTICUS *43:27-28* [RSV]

HE IS THE ALL

FOR HE IS GREATER THAN ALL HIS WORKS

AM very dark, but comely,
  O daughters of Jerusalem,
like the tents of Kedar,
  like the curtains of Solomon.

I am a rose of Sharon,
  a lily of the valleys.

*A*s a lily among brambles,
  so is my love among maidens.

*A*s an apple tree among the trees of
the wood,
  so is my beloved among young men.
With great delight I sat in his shadow,
  and his fruit was sweet to my taste.
He brought me to the banqueting house,
  and his banner over me was love.
Sustain me with raisins,
  refresh me with apples;
  for I am sick with love.

THE SONG OF SOLOMON *1:5; 2:1-5* [RSV]

PON my bed by night
I sought him whom my soul loves;
I sought him, but found him not;
    I called him, but he gave no answer.
"I will rise now, and go about the city,
    in the streets and in the squares;
I will seek him whom my soul loves."
    I sought him, but found him not.
The watchmen found me, as they went
about in the city.
    "Have you seen him whom my soul
loves?"
Scarcely had I passed them,
    when I found him whom my soul loves.
I held him, and would not let him go
    until I had brought him into my
mother's house,
    and into the chamber of her that
conceived me. ⤎

THE SONG OF SOLOMON *3:1-4* [RSV]

OU have ravished my heart, my sister,
my bride,
   you have ravished my heart
   with a glance of your eyes,
   with one jewel of your necklace.
How sweet is your love, my sister, my bride!
   how much better is your love than wine,
   and the fragrance of your oils than
any spice!
Your lips distil nectar, my bride;
   honey and milk are under your tongue;
   the scent of your garments is like the scent
of Lebanon.
A garden locked is my sister, my bride,
   a garden locked, a fountain sealed.
Your shoots are an orchard of pomegranates,
   with all choicest fruits,
   henna with nard,
nard and saffron, calamus and cinnamon,
   with all trees of frankincense,
   myrrh and aloes, with all chief spices -
a garden fountain, a well of living water,
   and flowing streams from Lebanon. ←

THE SONG OF SOLOMON 4:9-15 [RSV]

HOW SWEET IS YOUR LOVE

A WELL OF LIVING WATER

o whom then will ye liken God,
or what likeness compare
with him? ... ←

*H*ave you not known? Have you
not heard?

Has it not been told you from the
beginning?

Have you not understood from the
foundations of the earth?
It is he who sits above the circle of
the earth,

and its inhabitants are like grasshoppers;
who stretches out the heavens
like a curtain,

and spreads them like a tent to dwell in;
who brings princes to nought,

and makes the rulers of the earth
as nothing. ←

*S*carcely are they planted, scarcely sown,
   scarcely has their stem taken root in
the earth,
when he blows upon them, and they
wither,
   and the tempest carries them off like
stubble. ↢

*T*o whom then will you compare me,
   that I should be like him? says the
Holy One. ↢

ISAIAH *40:18; 21-25* [RSV]

FOR my thoughts are not
your thoughts,
neither are your ways my ways, says the
LORD.
For as the heavens are higher than the
earth,
    so are my ways higher than your ways
    and my thoughts than your thoughts.
For as the rain and the snow come
down from heaven,
    and return not thither but water
the earth,
making it bring forth and sprout,
    giving seed to the sower and bread to
the eater,
so shall my word be that goes forth from
my mouth;
    it shall not return to me empty,
but it shall accomplish that which
I purpose,
    and prosper in the thing for which I
sent it."

ISAIAH 55:8-11 [RSV]

GOD WILL BE YOUR GLORY

O LORD, thou art our Father;
we are the clay, and thou art
our potter; and we are all the work of
thy hand. ✦

*Th*en I went down to the potter's
house, and, behold, he wrought a work
on the wheels. And the vessel that he
made of clay was marred in the hand of
the potter: so he made it again another
vessel, as seemed good to the potter to
make it. ✦

ISAIAH *64:8*; JEREMIAH *18:3-4* [AV]

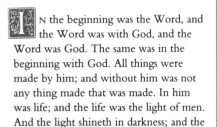

I N the beginning was the Word, and the Word was with God, and the Word was God. The same was in the beginning with God. All things were made by him; and without him was not any thing made that was made. In him was life; and the life was the light of men. And the light shineth in darkness; and the darkness comprehended it not... ✦

*Th*at was the true Light, which lighteth every man that cometh into the world. He was in the world, and the world was made by him, and the world knew him not. He came unto his own, and his own received him not. But as many as received him, to them gave he power to become the sons of God, even to them that believe on his name: which were born, not of blood, nor of the will of the flesh, nor of the will of man, but of God. ✦

JOHN 1:1-5, 9-13 [AV]

BLESSED are the poor in spirit: for theirs is the kingdom of heaven.

Blessed are they that mourn: for they shall be comforted.

Blessed are the meek: for they shall inherit the earth.

Blessed are they which do hunger and thirst after righteousness: for they shall be filled.

Blessed are the merciful: for they shall obtain mercy.

Blessed are the pure in heart: for they shall see God.

Blessed are the peacemakers: for they shall be called the children of God.

Blessed are they which are persecuted for righteousness' sake: for theirs is the kingdom of heaven. ✦

MATTHEW 5:3-10 [AV]

LAY not up for yourselves treasures upon earth, where moth and rust doth corrupt, and where thieves break through and steal: but lay up for yourselves treasures in heaven, where neither moth nor rust doth corrupt, and where thieves do not break through nor steal: for where your treasure is, there will your heart be also. ←

MATTHEW 6:19-21 [AV]

AVE faith in God. For verily I say unto you, That whosoever shall say unto this mountain, Be thou removed, and be thou cast into the sea; and shall not doubt in his heart, but shall believe that those things which he saith shall come to pass; he shall have whatsoever he saith. Therefore I say unto you, What things soever ye desire, when ye pray, believe that ye receive them, and ye shall have them. ←

MARK *11:22-24* [AV]

HEN you pray, go into your room and shut the door and pray to your Father who is in secret; and your Father who sees in secret will reward you ...for your Father knows what you need before you ask him. Pray then like this:

Our Father who art in heaven,
Hallowed be thy name.
Thy kingdom come.
Thy will be done,
On earth as it is in heaven.
Give us this day our daily bread,
And forgive us our debts,
As we also have forgiven our debtors;
And lead us not into temptation,
But deliver us from evil.
For thine is the kingdom
And the power and the glory,
for ever. Amen. ✦

MATTHEW 6:6, 8-13 [RSV]

D o not be anxious about your life, what you shall eat or what you shall drink, nor about your body, what you shall put on. Is not life more than food, and the body more than clothing? Look at the birds of the air: they neither sow nor reap nor gather into barns, and yet your heavenly Father feeds them. Are you not of more value than they? And which of you by being anxious can add one cubit to his span of life? And why are you anxious about clothing? Consider the lilies of the field, how they grow; they neither toil nor spin; yet I tell you, even Solomon in all his glory was not arrayed like one of these. But if God so clothes the grass of the field, which today is alive and tomorrow is thrown into the oven, will he not much more clothe you, O men of little faith? Therefore do not be anxious, saying,

'What shall we eat?' or 'What shall we drink?' or 'What shall we wear?' For the Gentiles seek all these things; and your heavenly Father knows that you need them all. But seek first his kingdom and his righteousness, and all these things shall be yours as well. ←

*T*herefore do not be anxious about tomorrow, for tomorrow will be anxious for itself. Let the day's own trouble be sufficient for the day. ←

MATTHEW 6:25-34 [RSV]

SK, and it shall be given you; seek, and ye shall find; knock, and it shall be opened unto you: for every one that asketh receiveth; and he that seeketh findeth; and to him that knocketh it shall be opened. Or what man is there of you, whom if his son ask bread, will he give him a stone? Or if he ask a fish, will he give him a serpent? If ye then, being evil, know how to give good gifts unto your children, how much more shall your Father which is in heaven give good things to them that ask him? ←

MATTHEW 7:7-11 | AV |

ASK AND IT SHALL BE GIVEN YOU

SEEK AND YE SHALL FIND

HE kingdom of heaven is like to a grain of mustard seed, which a man took, and sowed in his field: which indeed is the least of all seeds: but when it is grown, it is the greatest among herbs, and becometh a tree, so that the birds of the air come and lodge in the branches thereof. ↚

The kingdom of heaven is like unto leaven, which a woman took, and hid in three measures of meal, till the whole was leavened. ↚

The kingdom of heaven is like unto a merchant man, seeking goodly pearls: who, when he had found one pearl of great price, went and sold all that he had, and bought it. ↚

MATTHEW 13:31-32; 13:33; 13:45-46 [AV]

IT is your Father's good pleasure to give you the kingdom. Sell that ye have, and give alms; provide yourselves bags which wax not old, a treasure in the heavens that faileth not, where no thief approacheth, neither moth corrupteth. For where your treasure is, there will your heart be also. Let your loins be girded about, and your lights burning; and ye yourselves like unto men that wait for their lord, when he will return from the wedding; that when he cometh and knocketh, they may open unto him immediately. ←

LUKE *12:32-36* [AV]

ERILY, verily, I say unto thee, Except a man be born of water and of the Spirit, he cannot enter into the kingdom of God. That which is born of the flesh is flesh; and that which is born of the Spirit is spirit. Marvel not that I said unto thee, Ye must be born again. The wind bloweth where it listeth, and thou hearest the sound thereof, but canst not tell whence it cometh, and whither it goeth: so is every one that is born of the Spirit. ←

JOHN 3:5-8 [AV]

 T is the spirit that gives life, the flesh is of no avail; the words that I have spoken to you are spirit and life. ←

JOHN 6:63 [RSV]

AM the light of the world: he that followeth me shall not walk in darkness, but shall have the light of life. ←

*Y*et a little while is the light with you. Walk while ye have the light, lest darkness come upon you: for he that walketh in darkness knoweth not whither he goeth. While ye have light, believe in the light, that ye may be children of light. ←

JOHN *8:12; 12:35* [AV]

I AM THE LIGHT OF THE WORLD

BELIEVE IN THE LIGHT

N my Father's house are many mansions: if it were not so, I would have told you. I go to prepare a place for you. And if I go and prepare a place for you, I will come again, and receive you unto myself; that where I am, there ye may be also. And whither I go ye know, and the way ye know. Thomas saith unto him, Lord, we know not whither thou goest; and how can we know the way? Jesus saith unto him, I am the way, the truth, and the life: no man cometh unto the Father, but by me. If ye had known me, ye should have known my Father also: and from henceforth ye know him, and have seen him. ←

JOHN 14:2-7 [AV]

I AM THE WAY, THE TRUTH, THE LIFE

I AM THE WAY, THE TRUTH, THE LIFE

N that day you will know that I am in my Father, and you in me, and I in you. ←

*T*he Counsellor, the Holy Spirit, whom the Father will send in my name, he will teach you all things, and bring to your remembrance all that I have said to you. Peace I leave with you, my peace I give to you: not as the world gives, do I give to you. ←

JOHN *14:20; 14:27* [RSV]

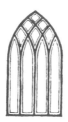

THE Lord is the Spirit, and where the Spirit of the Lord is, there is freedom. And we all, with unveiled face, reflecting the glory of the Lord, are being changed into his likeness from one degree of glory to another; for this comes from the Lord who is the Spirit. ✦

For our light affliction, which is but for a moment, worketh for us a far more exceeding and eternal weight of glory; while we look not at the things which are seen, but at the things which are not seen: for the things which are seen are temporal; but the things which are not seen are eternal. ✦

2 CORINTHIANS 3:17-18 | RSV |;
4:17-18 | AV |

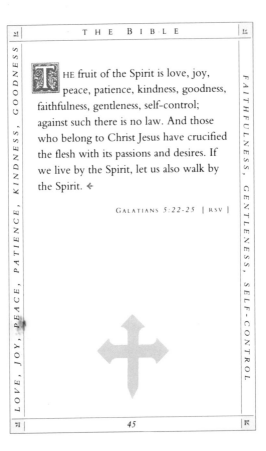

T HE fruit of the Spirit is love, joy, peace, patience, kindness, goodness, faithfulness, gentleness, self-control; against such there is no law. And those who belong to Christ Jesus have crucified the flesh with its passions and desires. If we live by the Spirit, let us also walk by the Spirit. ←

GALATIANS 5:22-25 | RSV |

LOVE, JOY, PEACE, PATIENCE, KINDNESS, GOODNESS

FAITHFULNESS, GENTLENESS, SELF-CONTROL

PERCEIVE that in every way you are very religious. For as I passed along, and observed the objects of your worship, I found also an altar with this inscription, 'To an unknown god.' What therefore you worship as unknown, this I proclaim to you. The God who made the world and every-thing in it, being Lord of heaven and earth, does not live in shrines made by man, nor is he served by human hands, as though he needed anything, since he himself gives to all men life and breath and everything. And he made from one every nation of men to live on all the

LORD OF HEAVEN AND EARTH

HE HIMSELF GIVES TO ALL MEN LIFE

face of the earth, having determined allotted periods and the boundaries of their habitation, that they should seek God, in the hope that they might feel after him, and find him. Yet he is not far from each one of us, for

'In him we live and move and have our being';
as even some of your poets have said,

'For we are indeed his offspring.'
Being then God's offspring, we ought not to think that the Deity is like gold or silver, or stone, a representation by the art and imagination of man. ←

ACTS *17:23-29* [RSV]

NOW ye not that ye are the temple of God, and that the Spirit of God dwelleth in you?. ✦

...*T*herefore glorify God in your body, and in your spirit, which are God's. ✦

*S*o, whether you eat or drink, or whatever you do, do all to the glory of God. ✦

1 CORINTHIANS 3:16 [AV];
6:20 [AV]; 10:31 [RSV]

DRAW near to God, and he will draw near to you. ←

JAMES 4:8 [RSV]

SET your affection on things above, not on things on the earth. ←

COLOSSIANS 3:2-3 [AV]

THE wisdom that is from above is first pure, then peaceable, gentle, and easy to be intreated, full of mercy and good fruits, without partiality, and without hypocrisy. And the fruit of righteousness is sown in peace of them that make peace. ←

JAMES 3:17-18 [AV]

DRAW NEAR TO GOD

AND HE WILL DRAW NEAR TO YOU

WHATSOEVER things are true, whatsoever things are honest, whatsoever things are just, whatsoever things are pure, whatsoever things are lovely, whatsoever things are of good report; if there be any virtue, and if there be any praise, think on these things. ↤

PHILIPPIANS 4:8 [AV]

TO the pure all things are pure. ↤

TITUS 1:15 [RSV]

DRAW NEAR TO GOD

AND HE WILL DRAW NEAR TO YOU

Now faith is the substance of things hoped for, the evidence of things not seen. For by it the elders obtained a good report. Through faith we understand that the worlds were framed by the word of God, so that things which are seen were not made of things which do appear. ←

HEBREWS *11:1-3* | AV |

BEFORE faith came, we were kept under the law, shut up unto the faith which should afterwards be revealed. Wherefore the law was our schoolmaster to bring us unto Christ, that we might be justified by faith. But after that faith is come, we are no longer under a schoolmaster.

For ye are all the children of God by faith in Christ Jesus. For as many of you as have been baptized into Christ have put on Christ. There is neither Jew nor Greek, there is neither bond nor free, there is neither male nor female: for ye are all one in Christ Jesus. ←

GALATIANS 3:23-28 [AV]

THERE IS NEITHER JEW NOR GREEK

THERE IS NEITHER BOND NOR FREE

F God is for us, who is against us? ←

ROMANS 8:31 [RSV]

AM persuaded, that neither death, nor life, nor angels, nor principalities, nor powers, nor things present, nor things to come, nor height, nor depth, nor any other creature, shall be able to separate us from the love of God, which is in Christ Jesus our Lord. ←

ROMANS 8:38-39 [AV]

here is one body, and one Spirit, even as ye are called in one hope of your calling; one Lord, one faith, one baptism, one God and Father of all, who is above all, and through all, and in you all. ←

EPHESIANS 4:4-6 [AV]

IF I speak in the tongues of men and of angels, but have not love, I am a noisy gong or a clanging cymbal. And if I have prophetic powers and understand all mysteries and all knowledge, and if I have all faith, so as to remove mountains, but have not love, I am nothing. If I give away all I have, and if I deliver my body to be burned, but have not love, I gain nothing.

Love is patient and kind; love is not jealous or boastful; it is not arrogant or rude. Love does not insist on its own way; it is not irritable or resentful; it does not rejoice at wrong, but rejoices in the right. Love bears all things, believes all things, hopes all things, endures all things. ←

LOVE IS PATIENT AND KIND

LOVE IS NOT JEALOUS OR BOASTFUL

Love never ends; as for prophecies, they will pass away; as for tongues, they will cease; as for knowledge, it will pass away. For our knowledge is imperfect and our prophecy is imperfect; but when the perfect comes the imperfect will pass away.

When I was a child, I spake as a child, I understood as a child, I thought as a child: but when I became a man, I put away childish things. For now we see through a glass, darkly; but then face to face: now I know in part; but then shall I know even as also I am known.

So faith, hope, love abide, these three; but the greatest of these is love. ←

1 CORINTHIANS *13:1-10* [RSV],
11-12 [AV], *13* [RSV]

ET love be without dissimulation. Abhor that which is evil; cleave to that which is good. Be kindly affectioned one to another with brotherly love; in honour preferring one another; not slothful in business; fervent in spirit; serving the Lord; rejoicing in hope; patient in tribulation; continuing instant in prayer; distributing to the necessity of saints; given to hospitality. ←

ROMANS *12:9-13* [AV]

O not neglect to show hospitality to strangers, for thereby some have entertained angels unawares. ←

HEBREWS *13:2* [RSV]

SERVING THE LORD

REJOICING IN HOPE

GOD is love; and he that dwelleth in love dwelleth in God, and God in him. Herein is our love made perfect, that we may have boldness in the day of judgment: because as he is, so are we in this world. There is no fear in love; but perfect love casteth out fear: because fear hath torment. He that feareth is not made perfect in love. We love him, because he first loved us. If a man say, I love God, and hateth his brother, he is a liar: for he that loveth not his brother whom he hath seen, how can he love God whom he hath not seen? ←

1 JOHN *4:16-20* [AV]

GOD IS LOVE

THERE IS NO FEAR IN LOVE

John...was in the isle that is called Patmos, for the word of God, and for the testimony of Jesus Christ. I was in the Spirit on the Lord's day, and heard behind me a great voice, as of a trumpet, saying, I am Alpha and Omega, the first and the last: and What thou seest write in a book... ←

REVELATION 1:9-11 [AV]

AND there appeared a great wonder in heaven; a woman clothed with the sun, and the moon under her feet, and upon her head a crown of twelve stars: and she being with child cried, travailing in birth, and pained to be delivered. And there appeared another wonder in heaven; and behold a great red dragon, having seven heads and ten horns, and seven crowns upon his heads. And his tail drew the third part of the stars of heaven, and did cast them down to the earth: and the dragon stood before the woman which was ready to be delivered, for to devour her child as soon as it was born. And she brought forth a man child, who was to rule all nations with a rod of iron: and her child was caught up unto God and to his throne. ⬦

REVELATION *12:1-5* [AV]

ND I saw an angel come down from heaven, having the key of the bottomless pit and a great chain in his hand. And he laid hold on the dragon, that old serpent, which is the Devil, and Satan, and bound him a thousand years, and cast him into the bottomless pit, and shut him up, and set a seal upon him, that he should deceive the nations no more, till the thousand years should be fulfilled: and after that he must be loosed a little season. ←

REVELATION 20:1-3 [AV]

 ND I saw a new heaven and a new earth: for the first heaven and the first earth were passed away; and there was no more sea. And I John saw the holy city, new Jerusalem, coming down from God out of heaven, prepared as a bride adorned for her husband.

And I heard a great voice out of heaven saying, Behold, the tabernacle of God is with men, and he will dwell with them, and they shall be his people, and God himself shall be with them, and be their God. And God shall wipe away all tears from their eyes; and there shall be no more death, neither sorrow, nor crying, neither shall there be any more pain: for the former things are passed away. And he that sat upon the throne said, Behold, I make all things new. And he said unto me, Write: for these words are true and faithful. And he said unto me, It is done. I am Alpha and Omega, the beginning and the end. I will give unto him that is athirst of the fountain of the water of life freely. He that overcometh shall inherit all things; and I will be his God, and he shall be my son. ←

REVELATION 21:1-7 [AV]

ND he shewed me a pure river of water of life, clear as crystal, proceeding out of the throne of God and of the Lamb. In the midst of the street of it, and on either side of the river, was there the tree of life, which bare twelve manner of fruits, and yielded her fruit every month: and the leaves of the tree were for the healing of the nations. And there shall be no more curse: but the throne of God and of the Lamb shall be in it; and his servants shall serve him: and they shall see his face; and his name shall be in their foreheads. And there shall be no night there; and they need no candle, neither light of the sun; for the Lord God giveth them light: and they shall reign for ever and ever. ←

REVELATION *22:1-5* [AV]

AND THERE SHALL BE NO MORE CURSE

THE LORD GOD GIVETH THEM LIGHT

ND he saith unto me...And, behold, I come quickly; and my reward is with me, to give every man according as his work shall be. I am Alpha and Omega, the beginning and the end, the first and the last. Blessed are they that do his commandments, that they might have right to the tree of life, and may enter in through the gates into the city. ←

REVELATION *22:10A, 12-14* [AV]

ND the Spirit and the bride say, Come. And let him that heareth say, Come. And let him that is athirst come. And whosoever will, let him take the water of life freely. ←

REVELATION *22:17* [AV]

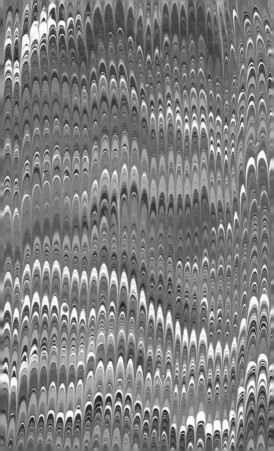